ISSUES OF IMMORTALITY

2020
Poems by
Elisavietta Ritchie

with illustrations
by Courtney Shelden

New Bay Books

Issues of Immortality

Poems by Elisavietta Ritchie

Copyright © 2021
by New Bay Books

Editor
Sandra Olivetti Martin
New Bay Books
Fairhaven, Maryland

NewBayBooks@gmail.com

www.newbaybooks.com

Title illustration: "Cover Birds" by Courtney Shelden
Interior Illustration: Birds by Courtney Shelden

Page 11: photo of Elisavietta Ritchie in Stockholm
by Alexander Farnsworth

Design by Suzanne Shelden
Shelden Studios
Prince Frederick, Maryland

www.sheldenstudios.com

Library of Congress Cataloging-in-Publication Data

ISBN   978-1-7348866-1-0

Printed in the United States of America
First Edition

WITH LOVE,
TO CLYDE HENRI FARNSWORTH

DEDICATION

To my unknown half-sister in Morocco, engendered early in World War II, when my dashing father—then a major—was stationed in Morocco. In his V-mail home, he wrote how he was billeted with a local "old Moroccan housewife." Years later, searching something else in the attic of our Washington, D.C. house on Macomb Street, a little photo slipped from an old passport: a beautiful girl. My father told me—"but not your mother"—that this was indeed his former housekeeper and that he sired a baby there: So I had a half-sister in Morocco. He sent money there for years.

So we half-sisters have grown up but forever unknown to each other and to the world. I can only imagine she has enjoyed a serious education and prospered all these years in Morocco.

Issues of Immortality

FOREWORD

Dear Reader:

Elisavietta Ritchie has a word for it. Many of us mortals struggle to find the words for what we want to say. Even journalists, who live by the word, have been convicted of writing "I can't find the words to express . . ."

Elisavietta is the exception. Words come to her as amply—and as evocatively—as stars to the night sky. As ancient night-watchers arranged the stars into constellations they knew by name, Elisavietta shapes her words into poems.

Her fluency gives her the gift of capturing the observation that, without words, might fleet by.

> *Nothing to park beneath,*
> *these untested moons.*
> *Might scrape a jagged*
> *mountaintop*
> *and pop*
> *or fall in uncharted seas—*

She describes feelings that echo in the heart or gut inchoately if we lack the words to call them by name and nature.

> *Does a bird live long enough*
> *to die of old age?*
> *What about us, o what?*

Words empower her to integrate travels through time and space—the journeys we all make in dreams and imaginings—into the fabric of everyday life.

> *The new moon sashays*
>   *into my slice of sky*
> *no longer can I dream of sleep*
> *but ride the tides of night*
> *to beach in some far reach*
> *of this night's universe*
> *what foreign shores*

Elisavictta's poems give the delicious sense that she is sharing secrets no one has thought before. They seem as well and naturally made as the leaf of a fern or flight of a tern.

Yet poems are not quite like amber. They do not sit timeless and undisturbed. Poets are notorious revisers, and in this compulsion Elisavietta is no exception. Drafts, as she tells us in her preface "may go on for years," until each unique word is in its perfect place—or as near as can be given publication schedules.

Of these she has met many—and is always trying for more. It is not plain vanity that drives such a compulsion. Elisavietta needs you to hear (for though a poem may rise to the eye, it always sounds in the ear) what she has written or else her words have gone nowhere. A poem unheard is like a bridge that's never built.

Reaching readers is why, when I was editor at New Bay Times newspaper, where I first knew Elisavietta, stories often brought to my mailbox a poem to continue the dialogue. It is why she has published 26 books of poems and stories. *Issues of Immortality* makes 27.

It is a small book of poems that came to be in 2020. Their common themes, as you can tell by the title, are life, love and loss. Suitably, in this year of the pandemic.

It is a deliberately small book, finite like a box of fine chocolates—in part so you will always wish for another. The poems are short for the same reason. They are deep and rich and will give you plenty to savor.

Sandra Olivetti Martin

Sandra Olivetti Martin
Editor
Fairhaven Cliffs, Maryland

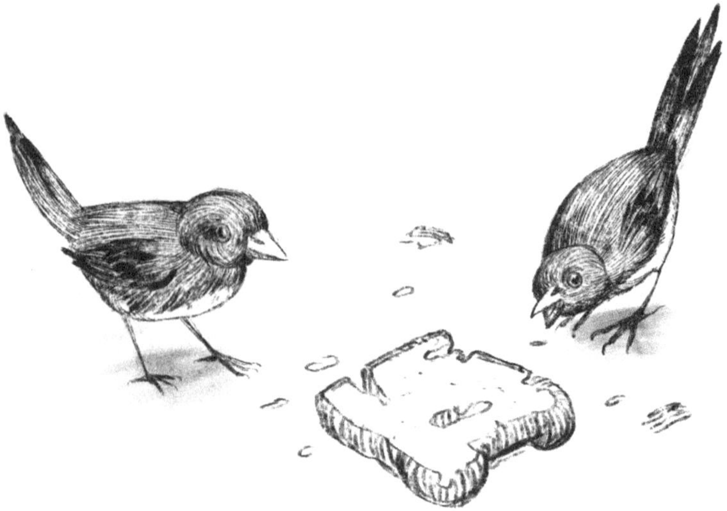

TABLE OF CONTENTS

Preface 11

I

Word Games 15
Issues of Immortality 16
Rags and Scraps 18
Annunciation 19
Weather Report 20

II

By 80, Poets Are Supposed to Croak 22
In Brief, Everything 23
Just a Stop-and-Go Moon 24
Sooty, or Aflame with Colors 25
When You Can't Get Out
    of Emptying Trash 26

III

Imperfections of This Osprey Feather 28
All Night I Wander 29
Storm Warnings: Wind Rising, High Tide .. 30
Visitations: Lunar 31
Why I Missed a Ride to the Workshop 32

IV

At Moonrise I Write Lives 34
Like Emily Dickinson 35
"Damn Drunks!" She Called Them 36
Battlefields, Legacies 37
Moon Check, Room Check: Midnight 38

V

Zipping through Lists 40
Going the Distance 41
Catch-and-Release Policy 42
The Value of Being a Writer
    When Indulging in Secret Affairs 44
Durability Warranty 45

VI

Comes a Time when Friends 48
Dead Robin on the Picnic Table 50
Time Stopped in Our Absence 51
The Bear at the Farm Market 52
One More Thing— 53

About the Author 55
Books and Chapbooks by the Author 58

PREFACE

"Write an author's statement," said Sandra Olivetti Martin, editor and publisher.

I don't set out to make poems or statements. Poems just come, unbidden as colds, are scribbled on whatever scrap of paper, laundry list, patch of sand or on water, merely the first of several drafts which may go back years.

W.H. Auden, invited for tea or dinner, was known to go to his host's shelves, reach for his own books, and to everyone's horror, edit them.

I too.

I will take my laptop or whatever paper, pencil, penknife and clay tablet to my grave or pyramid or cloud.

—Elisavietta Ritchie

I

Word Games

At this point words
are multisyllabic
to ward off
monosyllabic death

So as when picking
blackberries among
poison ivy and thorns
up the muddy lane
through the swamp

let us choose
the ripe with care
Avoid the thorns

Issues of Immortality

If poets are indeed immortal
we will live forever in our pyramids
beyond the River Styx.

Yet how to smuggle out
our latest manuscripts?
Entrance blocks too big to budge.

Those sleek tomb cats as couriers?
Unreliable, distractible, they ate
our carrier pigeons. Still,
    they chase the mice.

Where are the hands that wrote
    our lusty poems?
Where the lovers who stoked
    our eager muse?
Our bones would clatter now
    as we embraced ...

Issues of Immortality

How to recite our work?
Tongues tangle in silk shrouds.
Lost teeth search for mouths.

Eyeballs bounce across
    this dusty floor.
Our ears snap off.
Laptops cannot find laps.

Sandstorms blow our scrolls away.
The power to communicate
must rely on extrasensory skills.

Still, we scratch our work
    on sooty walls,
carve hieroglyphs in sand,
scribble on the tricky Styx ...

Rags and Scraps

All day I have not written
All night I cannot sleep

Not one blank sheet of paper
But here's a laundry list

Panties bras socks sheets
Will provide verisimilitude ...

Sweeter than cough syrup
my last inch of Amaretto yields

details of color, heft and taste
Might tumble me

into the mid-plot of a dream
yield this night's invention

At school I was the first to find
a smuggled *Forever Amber*

Annunciation

The redheaded red-shouldered
song sparrow lands
on our balcony rail three flights up.

With a message?
Warning about the end
    of the world?
The fate of lost stars? Or simply:

Where are my crumbs?
I hasten to crunch,
scatter my toast

Weather Report

Dead calm now, but you know
the hurricane is due.

Still, you rig the jib, cast off,
set sail from the harbor,

steer, sails full, past bouncing lights
on buoys until the wind—

The wind! the wind! More wind!
Best change course, return

toward fixed lights onshore,
the port, your pier, the floating dock—

But the pier is ripped apart—
Tethered boats break from
    their moorings—

All swept away in the hurricane
you knew was due—

Still, you set sail—

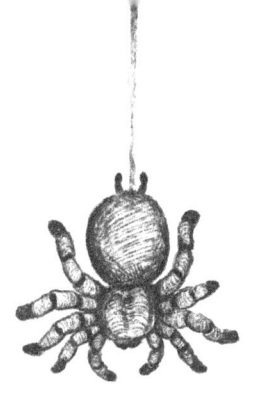

II

By 80, Poets Are Supposed to Croak
[cease cluttering the continents with words]

Still words glitter forth like aging
whores on back streets of our lives,
perform whatever tricks we ask,
for money or for free.

Dear antique gods of poetry
you hang around off stage
battle scars forever raw,

You understand iniquities
if not the impotence of age.
We pray you will take pity
on our faltering feet.

In Brief, Everything

That touches us
may kill us

little by little or
blessedly instantly

Warnings are out
can't miss them

A giant spider ate
a possum in Australia

A panther nabbed
a baby bear Miami

We wind around
this mountain road

May slip
Off

Just a Stop-and-Go Moon

Nothing to park beneath,
these untested moons.
Might scrape a jagged
mountaintop
and pop
or fall in uncharted seas—

Yet several nights before
the moon risks
FULL
even if clouds mask the sky
my energy soars

I write—

Sooty, or Aflame with Colors

Too gaudy for decent people
birds fly into my life, perch
on the balcony, announce

no further miraculous births
just twitter about
a few knock-ups.

Birds akin to angels
I set out biscuit crumbs,
do not demand credentials.

When You Can't Get Out of Emptying Trash

into the can in the alley
and back in the flat
you rinse the waste basket

snap your briefcase
lock the door
toss keys in the passing truck

no more adventures here
you set off on a more fragrant
less dangerous path

flee to Los Angeles
(nothing to do with angels
or angles or tangles)

unsure you will ever return
sure that you won't

III

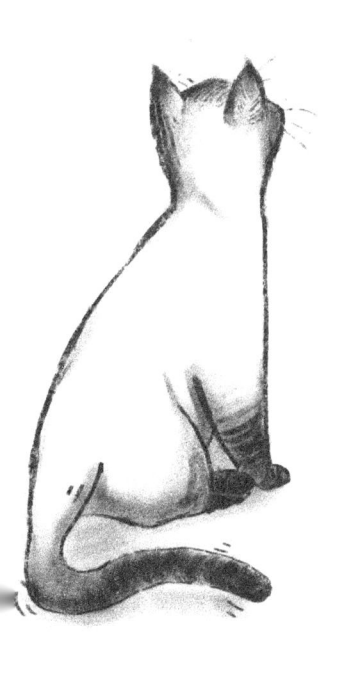

Imperfections of This Osprey Feather

striped gray and white
too ruffled
might have rooked
his flight

but fallen into my hands
must be a sign—

you too better fly right

Thrust in a coffee mug
with three other feathers
ergo a quartet

they wait to fly me
to a heaven
tired of waiting

but already overcrowded

I don't mind
waiting my turn
still so much to do

All Night I Wander

A half-baked moon reveals
black flies on windowsills

A sliver of brain reveals
black thoughts winged in, stuck

By the imperfect light
Still, I can write

Storm Warnings: Wind Rising, High Tide—

Swans in the inlet,
ospreys in the air,
gulls everywhere,
all vanish to calmer coves.

I run to the dock,
leap aboard
    the bucking sailboat,
bail last night's deluge
from the sloshing bilge.

Raise and cleat the sails,
check halyards, lines,
cast off from the dock,
head for the mouth
    of the harbor—
Off to chart new seas:
Every sail could be our last.

Visitations: Lunar

The new moon sashays
    into my slice of sky
no longer can I dream of sleep
but ride the tides of night
to beach in some far reach
of this night's universe
what foreign shores

Why I Missed a Ride to the Workshop

After another insomniac night
at dawn I slept.

The obsidian cat with emerald eyes
slept too.

In her dreams she nibbled, then
ate my poem even as I was rewriting.

She yawns—her teeth mini-scimitars—
curls back into her dreams, leaves

wisps of black hair on my white quilt,
wisps of words in the air …

IV

At Moonrise
I Write Lives

Moon rays play on faces
of my ancestors
or someone else's

They all show up
alive or not

Glad to welcome
these new neighbors
I set out teacups

thimble glasses
for the stronger stuff
to jolt them back

May fireflies
light their way

Like Emily Dickinson

A desperate search for paper
though none, we know, is left

so like Emily I write
on envelopes in the dark

At sunrise will I decipher
what may be a sonnet or

the grocery list forgotten
at the store

"Damn Drunks!" She Called Them

Those neighbors huddled at the bar
whose names she could not remember

I was thirteen when I realized
why my mother pioneer professional
known for her generosity

always staggered off to bed at only seven,
full ashtrays and empty bottles stashed

My Lesson 101 in ironies, hypocrisies,
example for my own double lives

Battlefields, Legacies

Must keep up my limp
across this field of Maryland corn ...

I think of my unknown uncle Ivan
in old St. Petersburg age nineteen
filling notebooks with his poems

Come the Russian Revolution
Ivan in the White Army
ever driven farther south

As his unit fought its way across
the corn fields beyond Poltava
he was shot and killed

Years later a Russian émigré group
gave him a posthumous medal

As I push stalks aside to cross
this field of corn, I like to think
he willed his soul to me

(Slavs can write of souls)

Current travel guides to Russia write
the fields around Poltava now
are city blocks

Moon Check, Room Check: Midnight

What goes on in rooms
down the dimmed hall:
Someone waits for fever to spike,
another for the pulse to speed up
or stop.

I slip outdoors to watch
the mischievous moon
dodge mountaintops
then settle on the sea
and disappear.

So we.

But no more siphoning life
through a soggy straw!

Gulp life, drain the flask—

V

Zipping through Lists

I stumble on line breaks
as on burnt stumps
rewrite my life

Assignations in bulldozed cafés
chance encounters
love in the jungle
in a geography of lands

Writing rewriting
virtual tomes
skimmed lists of sins
recorded in semen and blood

Those who glimpse my words
may weigh
truth or invention
or both or none

What exists in the mind
is true as what may have
happened or not,
said Henri Bergson

Going the Distance

"You going the distance, honey, with me?"
asked the handsome professor, revving
his Harley. "We can hide out. I've a room ...

Unsure of his intimations of hospitality
and lust, I clung to his back while
we zoomed between Iowa cornfields

en route to his college where
I was to accept a prize
for my first poetry book.

"Too stoned to teach," he said on arrival ...
"Take over my class ... We'll meet tonight for
    ... ummmm ..."
The field of crows rose and flew out of sight.

I too slipped away ... But whenever I see
a Harley zooming between the fields of corn,
    I remember
his words, my missed opportunities ...

Catch-and-Release Policy

The Nature Conservancy sent me
their Certificate of Recognition
for Protection of Wildlife

What to do
with the dashing merman
in my big crab trap?

He looks at me
with soulful salty eyes,
bubbles on his chin.

He surely begs for freedom
in his strange language
punctuated with gurgles.

What a catch!
A keeper, though too big
for my frying pan.

I untangle him,
bring him home
to my small aquarium …

Is that wise? He'll scorn
dry fish food, demand
caviar from the Caspian.

Does he flick his scaly tail
        in his sleep?
Will his whiskers tickle?
We will find out,

We will find out …

The Value of Being a Writer When Indulging in Secret Affairs

My old professor read my books,

"What a femme fatale you are—
or were—
at least in your fiction ...
Did all that happen?
In your wild imagination?"

Better answer: *I've forgotten.*
Perhaps it's literary license.

He then invited me to visit while
his wife was off at work ...

How doubly rich our several lives
true-true and invented ...

Durability Warranty

> *Those you once loved*
> *You love forever.*
> *—Konstantin Simonov*

I've outlived old lovers
They bore our secrets
to their far-flung graves

I will to mine.
Old spouses and friends
will stay ignorant.

If we die at sea, toss us overboard,
to circulate the globe forever as
torches of phosphorescence

light our muted way
through humid seas,
melt icebergs at the poles.

On heaven's beaches
we'll spread our picnic and
have a blast.

VI

Comes a Time when Friends

are made and met only on Facebook
shared online in Majorca while you seek
a pop artist FRIEND on Malta

In the hospital lobby to say Farewell Friend
to a cousin-by-marriage you've never met
No one else left to make The Arrangements

No empty chairs in WAITING everyone
      hides flasks
and Mason jars of yellowish liquid
under decade-old *Good Housekeepings*

Tired of receptionists painting their nails
while hunting your Social Security digits
you slip out through the crowded
      lobby through

the circle-in-circles door to the
      sloshing street
You lack cash airport pass destination
Wave for a taxi None stop

Issues of Immortality

A mud-coated pickup pauses
Driver never learned English
on his war-ravaged island fled yesterday

He drives beyond slums beyond woods
to a field with a dirty helicopter
no numbers no company name no fuel

Pushing aside vagrant cows the pilot
yanks you aboard but needs cash
for fuel coffee donuts rum gas *Buckle Up*

crackles in twenty archaic tongues
The helicopter rises over roiled surf
crowded with FRIENDS seeking FRIENDS

May we all meet in the FRIENDLY heavens
To picnic on the heavenly waterfront
Check your DEVICE to find where

Dead Robin on the Picnic Table

Shot? I think not:
too small to interest a shooter.

A cat would leave
claw prints, tooth marks.

Does a bird live long enough
to die of old age?

What about us, o what?

Time Stopped in Our Absence

After our travels we returned
to our house by the river
to find all our clocks askew.

They must have stopped
    in thunderstorms,
resumed on their own,
died many deaths in between.

We once thought we were in charge.

We too fluctuate with weather
    and travel,
adapt or don't. We pray for fair skies,
at least survival, but know how scant
our control over time and space ...

The Bear at the Farm Market

What does the bear do if the cart
he planned to rob of apples,
holds only poems?

Swipe and chew, masticate, digest.
He becomes literate as he eats the poems,
more so when he swallows the poet.

One More Thing—

We'll say as they
are hauling us off,
please wait—

One more thing
still undone
not even begun

Whatever words
to distract
the angel or devil

or burly grave digger
in charge of our disposal
Whoa! Hang on there!

Wait! One more thing
or two or three
before we croak—

Issues of Immortality

About the Author

Elisavietta Ritchie is a multi-tasking writer, poet, editor, photographer, mentor, workshop leader and poet-in-the-schools and universities in the United States and, sponsored by the United States Information Service, Brazil, Australia, Canada and the Far East.

She won the Great Lakes Colleges Award for her first book, *Tightening the Circle over Eel Country*; four National Endowment for the Arts, Pushcart and other awards; and many acceptances for individual poems and stories. She was asked for poems to be set to compositions by composers David Owens, Jackson Berkey and others.

She continues to write, mentor, host informal writers' workshops and to serve as an assistant editor to anthologies of poems on the Patuxent River watershed in Southern Maryland.

Elisavietta Ritchie and Donald Grady Shomette created an exhibit of his photographs and her poems several decades ago. They have come together again for the book *Navigational Hazards*.

Most recently, New Bay Books publisher Sandra Olivetti Martin invited her to create a collection of her recent poems, with book design by Suzanne Shelden.

Elisavietta Ritchie is married to writer and former *New York Times* journalist Clyde Henri Farnsworth, and frequently took photographs to accompany his articles in Canada, Australia, Europe and the United States. They live at the tip of Southern Maryland overlooking the Patuxent River. Both are insomniacs.

Issues of Immortality

Books and Chapbooks by the Author

NAVIGATIONAL HAZARDS, featuring the photography of Donald Shomette and the poetry of Elisavietta Ritchie—Wineberry Press (2020)

PAX: AN ANTHOLOGY OF SOUTHERN MARYLAND POETRY—Wineberry Press (2019) Special thanks to my fellow writers Doug Hile, Rocky Jones, Clyde Henri Farnsworth, Kate Lassman, Cliff Lynn, George Miller, Elspeth Cameron Ritchie, Suzanne Shelden, Carol Shomette, Donald Grady Shomette, Jeff Smallwood, Laura Stewart Webb, Joanne Van Wie.

LUNATIC MOONS: INSOMNIA CANTATAS—Shelden Studios (2019)

THE SCOTCH RUNNER: STORIES—Poets' Choice Publishers (2018)

HARBINGERS—Poets' Choice Publishers (2017)

REFLECTIONS: POEMS ON PAINTINGS, A POET'S GALLERY—Poets' Choice Publishers (2017)

BABUSHKA'S BEADS: A GEOGRAPHY OF GENES—Poets' Choice Publishers (2016)

GUY WIRES—Poets' Choice Publishers (2015)

IN HASTE I WRITE YOU THIS NOTE: STORIES & HALF STORIES—Washington Writers' Publishing House (print: 2000, e-book 2015)

TIGER UPSTAIRS ON CONNECTICUT AVENUE—Cherry Grove Collections, WordTech Communications (2013)

FEATHERS, OR, LOVE ON THE WING—Shelden Studios, collaboration with artists Megan Richard & Suzanne Shelden (2013)

FROM THE ARTIST'S DEATHBED—Winterhawk Press (chapbook, 2012)

CORMORANT BEYOND THE COMPOST—Cherry Grove Collections, WordTech Communications (2011)

REAL TOADS—Black Buzzard Press (chapbook, 2008)

AWAITING PERMISSION TO LAND—Cherry Grove Collections, WordTech Communications (2006)

THE SPIRIT OF THE WALRUS—Bright Hill Press (chapbook, 2005)

THE ARC OF THE STORM—Signal Books (1998)

ELEGY FOR THE OTHER WOMAN: NEW & SELECTED POEMS—Signal Books (1996)

WILD GARLIC: THE JOURNAL OF MARIA X. —Harper Collins (novel in verse, chapbook, 1995)

A WOUND-UP CAT AND OTHER BEDTIME STORIES—Palmerston Press (chapbook, 1993)

FLYING TIME: STORIES & HALF-STORIES— Signal Books (1986, 1988)

THE PROBLEM WITH EDEN— Armstrong State College Press (chapbook, 1985)

RAKING THE SNOW—Washington Writers' Publishing House (1982)

A SHEATH OF DREAMS & OTHER GAMES—Proteus Press (1976)

TIGHTENING THE CIRCLE OVER EEL COUNTRY—Acropolis Books (1974)

TIMBOT—The Lit Press (novella-in-verse, chapbook, first edition 1970) Poetry

Anthologies edited:

THE DOLPHIN'S ARC: POEMS ON ENDANGERED CREATURES OF THE SEA—SCOP (1986)

FINDING THE NAME—The Wineberry Press (1983)

Issues of Immortality